Brown Little Babies

A Book of Photos and Poems

Author and Illustrator: Evelyn Laurine Gresham

Print information available on the last page

Rev. date: 1/4/2019

To order additional copies of this book, contact:
Xlibris
1-888-795-4274
www.Xlibris.com
Orders@Xlibris.com

Dedication

I would like to give thanks to God for inspiring me to do this book. I would also like to thank my son David Mock for being my biggest fan. Lastly, I would like to thank all of my family and friends that gave me permission to use their pictures, love and blessings to you all!

"A Message From The Heart"

Babies, we must hold them and mold them.
We must gently lead them on the right path.
We must capture their sense of wonder and help keep it there.
We must train them and teach them to do the right thing, so
each baby will have a brighter future.

Evelyn Laurine Gresham

Brown Little Babies

"Brown Little Baby"

Brown little baby
fly like a bird

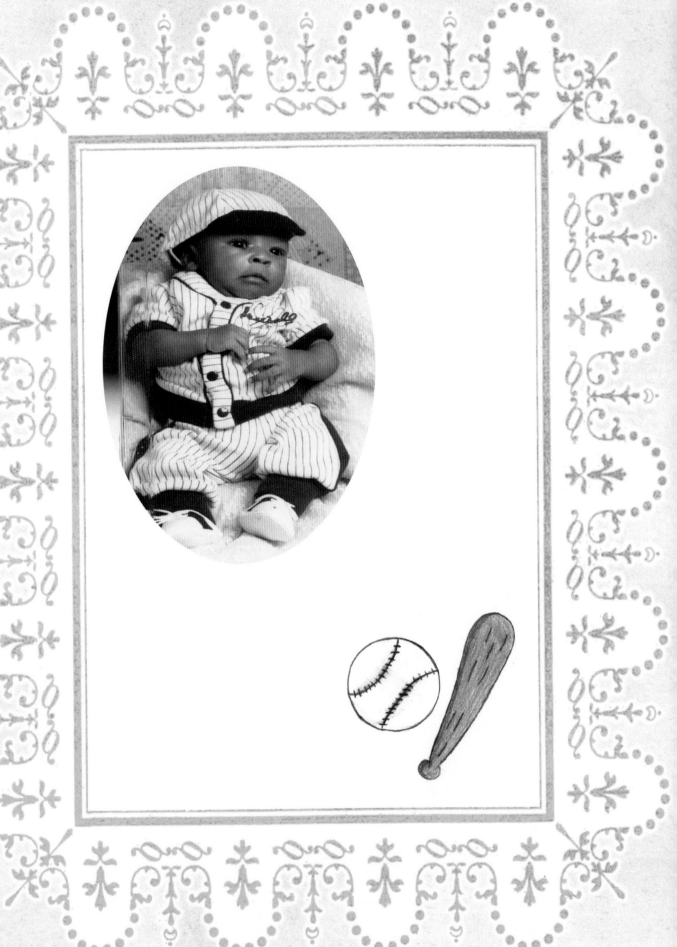

Brown little baby
has a story
that's never been heard

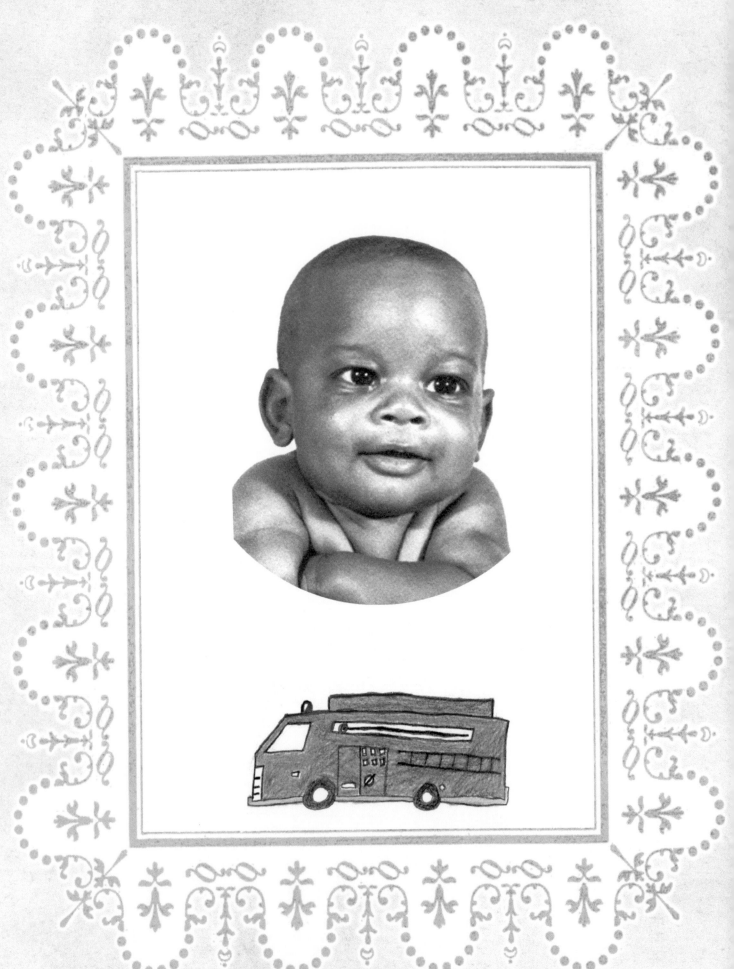

I was once a brown little baby
so cute, warm and round

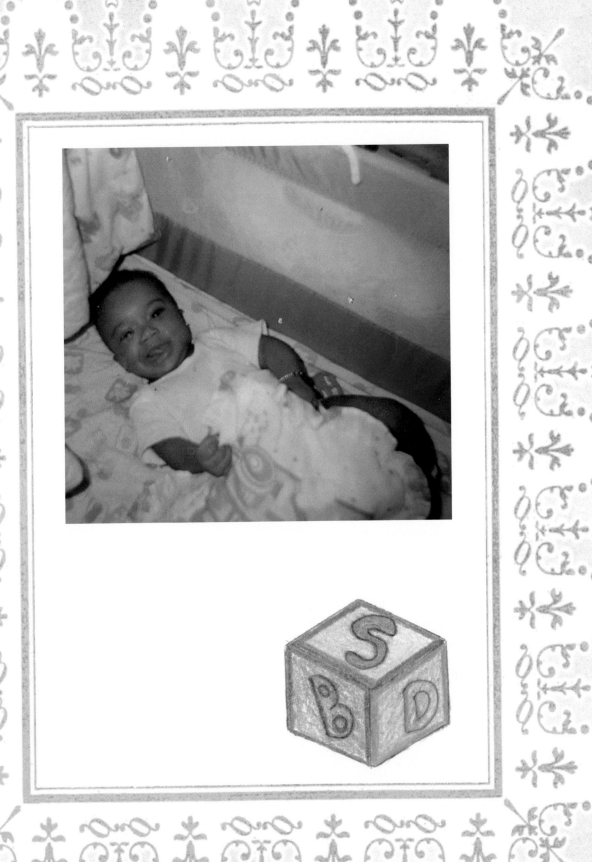

Here the giggles
the laughter
and the sound
as the baby wakes
and comes around

Brown little baby
cute, sweet and fine

Brown little baby
smiles all the time

Brown little baby
with curly waves
people see you
smile and start to rave

Those that have a brown little baby
are oh so proud
strutting their stuff
as they walk through the crowd

We give you thanks
for all your praise
and all the lovely things you say

We wish you all the best
with lots of
love and happiness

Brown little baby
oh so kind

Brown little babies
will last throughout time!

"Sweet Baby"

Sweet sweet baby
how do you do?

Sweet sweet baby
I love you

Sweet sweet baby
one, two, three
I chuckle and I chuckle
just for thee

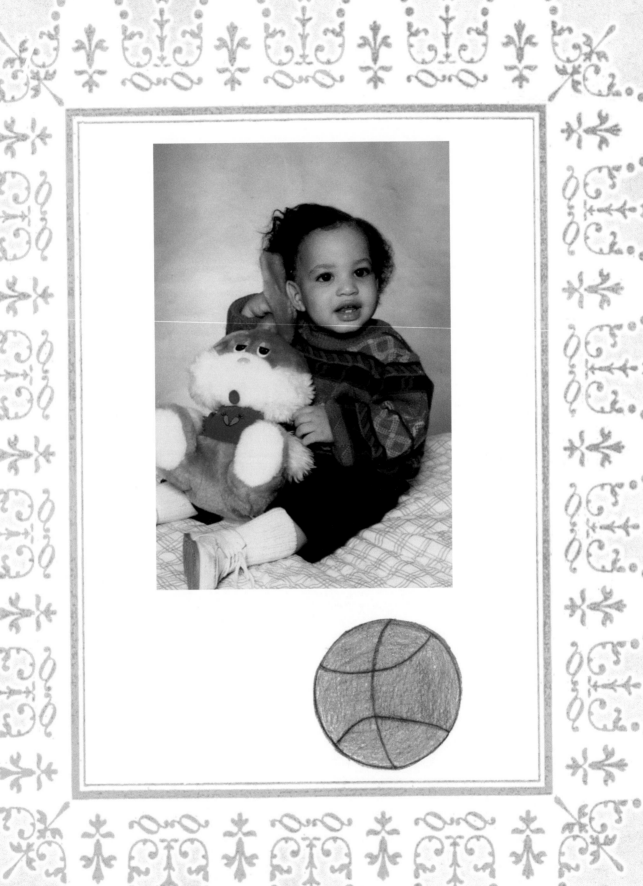

One plus one
makes two not three
sweet sweet baby
you're all that I need

Don't wave good-bye
just wave hello
sweet sweet baby
you're all that I know

"Taking A Bath"

Splish splash, splish splash
I love to take a bath
Bubbles floating in the air
water flying everywhere
splish splash, splish splash
I love to take a bath

"When I Was A Baby Girl"

When I was a baby girl
I had soft black hair
with lots of pretty curls!
I had tiny feet
that looked so neat!
I looked my best
in a white fancy dress
when I was a baby girl!

"Being Together"

Momma, I want to be with thee
sitting under the apple tree
reading a story or two to me
momma, I want to be with thee

Sitting on a stoop
laying my head in your lap
looking up into your big beautiful eyes
and wondering where it all lies

When your sad, lonely or full of glee
remember momma,
you'll always be special to me.

"Having A Baby Boy"

Having a baby boy
gives my heart lots of joy
Here is my son
his future he will run
Proud, smart, and strong!
But, for now my son
play and have fun
for the future will await you
when the time comes

About The Author

Evelyn Gresham has loved writing ever since she was a child. She spent most of her life writing poetry and children stories. This book is a tribute to all African American babies. Evelyn was born in Staten Island New York, but now lives in Magnolia New Jersey with her family.

The End